ANTI CORRUPTION

ANTI CORRUPTION IN SOCIETY

TAMANA TAMANA JAN

Anti-Corruption affects all areas of society. Preventing corruption unlocks progress towards the Sustainable Development Goals, helps protect our planet, creates jobs, achieves gender equality, and secures wider access to essential services such as healthcare and education

Corruption can have a devastating impact on the availability, quality and accessibility of human rights-related goods and services. Moreover, it undermines the functioning and legitimacy of institutions and processes, the rule of law and ultimately the State itself

Because corruption creates fiscal distortions and redirects money allocated to income grants, eligibility for housing or pensions and weakens service delivery, it is usually the poor who suffer most. Income inequality has increased in most countries experiencing high levels of corruption.

Corruption increases income inequality and poverty through lower economic growth; biased tax systems favoring the rich and well-connected; poor targeting of social programs; use of wealth by the well-to-do to lobby government for favorable policies that perpetuate inequality in asset ownership; lower social spending;

Contents

CHAPTER ONE

- **Anti-corruption** (or **anticorruption**) comprise activities that oppose or inhibit corruption. Just as corruption takes many forms, anti-corruption efforts vary in scope and in strategy. A general distinction between preventive and reactive measures is sometimes drawn. In such framework, investigative authorities and their attempts to unveil corrupt practices would be considered reactive, while education on the negative impact of corruption, or firm-internal compliance programs are classified as the former.

Anti-corruption collective action is a form of collective action with the aim of combatting corruption and bribery risks in public procurement. It is a collaborative anti-corruption activity that brings together representatives of the private sector, public sector and civil society.

Corruption is a phenomenon that has flooded throughout the world and what is does is stopping the natural growth of countries or regions. That's why it is also known as an all-pervading circumstance and unnecessary hindrance for countries that are striving to move forward. When there are fraudulent actions just because a person is in power, it is known as Corruption.

Corruption means practices or decisions taken that result in favorable solutions for lesser parties. When there is moral degradation, and no amount of honest valuation can make you realize that you have gone on the wrong path, it leads to Corruption. Lust for power and money often are the common reasons for Corruption. Corruption strips a person away from his character, and this leads to the deteriorating ability of duties. There are many political leaders of different countries who are involved in this, and it rapidly spreads to lower levels as well. Countries that are superpowers are also not immune to it.

Today, No country is immune to the disease of Corruption. All and every country takes part in it involuntarily because that is the key to unbelievable success and power. And power comes from the amount of money, so people morally degrade themselves and run in the wrong direction for cash. There may be a difference in the amount of Corruption in all the countries, but it exists all the same.

Public Life, Personal Life, Politics, administration, education, and even Research and security is also not immune to Corruption. There is hardly any exception. Corruption is suitably punished in other countries, but that is not the case in India, as there is no specific punishment for any Corruption. Corruption is an offence that not ruins lives but ruins families as well because once a person gets habituated to it no one but themselves can stop them from it.

There are many scams that are not included in the public eye but have impacted a lot. They are known as Corruption. Corruption is an act of treachery that has rarely left anyone or any place. From Hospitals to corporations and governments, nothing and no one is immune from Corruption. Corruption starts from the higher levels and moves down to the lower levels rapidly, forming an atmosphere of less hard work and cheated results.

There are even proofs that politicians were provided resources by drug lords and smugglers, and when they or their existence is threatened, immediate actions are taken against them mostly resulting in death. Even the most influential countries are not free from Corruption because who would not like power and success? And the easiest way to do that is by earning an excessive amount of money. Corruption stops them from degrading influence. However, Corruption cannot prevent the degradation of their morals or values, and it increases the same. None of us can even imagine the amount of money that goes into their accounts for personal accumulations. Corruption is now a bug that is insidious inside every Department and arena of the government. Corruption has now crippled our economy, and our functions have gone haywire due to it.

That" one cannot fight Corruption by fighting it" and this is entirely correct. Corruption means the act which stems from Lust or greed for money and going to any and every length needed to get illegal tasks done. Corruption is active in each and every part and country of the world. Corruption cannot be stopped or executed in any way. It can only be finished if it is inside a man's heart to stop it. There are many methods of Corruption, and the most common one is bribery.

Bribery means the tactic that is used for using favors or gifts for personal gain. There are different types of favors included in this. The other is embezzlement which means withholding assets which can be further used for theft. Usually, there are one or more persons involved who are entrusted with these assets, and it can also be called a financial fraud.

Extortion means to claim any assets, land or property illegally. Favoritism or Nepotism is also in full-fledged flow these days when only the favorite persons or direct relatives of those in power ascend into their potential. There are not many ways of stopping Corruption, but they do exist.

The government can give a better salary to their employees who are equivalent to the amount of work that they put in. Decreasing the workload and increasing workers can also be an excellent way to cease this influential and illegal practice. Strict Laws are needed for stopping this and the best way to compete; this is the way of putting guilty criminals to their End. The government can work to keep the inflation levels low in the country so they can work accordingly. Corruption cannot be fought against, and it can only be stopped.

Corruption, therefore, ranges in its manifestations from bribery and fraud to sociopolitical transformations of the greatest magnitude. Corruption, however, does not always lead to collapse. At times, corruption may be better conceived as a suboptimal way of getting things done when ethically superior ways are perceived as being unavailable, flawed, or too costly. Short of collapse, corruption can lead to a tenacious pattern of unethical behavior that is sustained and replicated over many years. This multiplicity of understandings suggests that corruption is a polyvalent concept. Naturally, it covers a variety of actions by a variety of actors in a variety of contexts. More importantly, from a definitional standpoint, different observers will characterize the same instance of corruption in different ways according to a variety of factors, including their values, assumptions, goals, cultures and skill sets. Accepting that there are different understandings of corruption and rising to this challenge can help us cultivate an integrated and multidisciplinary understanding of corruption. At the same time, it is important to ask: what kind of conduct could be causally associated with everything from dishonesty to the downfall of an empire or a political system?

The law is perhaps the best place to look for concrete definitions of corrupt actions. However, different legal standards also vary in their approach and implementation. Legal standards are known for their technical and complex formulations, and for their susceptibility to multiple interpretations at the hands of lawyers and judges. Domestic criminal laws articulate a reasonably concrete understanding of corrupt conduct, make that understanding binding on everyone in the national territory, and can impose punishment on offenders (for a discussion of national anti-corruption laws, see on Anti-Corruption. International conventions have taken this further, reflecting a consensus view on what constitutes corrupt behavior these conventions are discussed further in University Module Series on Anti-Corruption. One might think that such a consensus would be elusive, given the variety of histories, cultures and legal systems in the world.

Effects of corruption

The effects of corruption are wide-ranging. Some of these effects are fairly obvious, while others require explanation. They include

Economic loss and inefficiency

Although obtaining exact figures on the economic costs of corruption is difficult, a 2016 report from the International Monetary Fund (IMF) estimated the cost of bribery alone to be. This represents a total economic loss of approximately 2% of global GDP. And yet it does not take into account the economic cost of all other forms of corruption. Regarding fraud, money-laundering and tax evasion, for example, the thousands of leaked documents known as the (commonly referred to as the Panama Papers) exposed the vast economic implications of offshore entities for many nations and for economic inequality in general. Finally, beyond deadweight economic loss, there is economic inefficiency to consider. When jobs (or contracts) are given to people (or companies) who offer bribes or share a personal connection, this occurs to the detriment of competition. The result is that more qualified candidates and firms are turned down. The more widespread such practices are, the more inefficient the economy becomes. Corruption in developing countries may cause underdevelopment. This can occur when international economic and humanitarian initiatives are derailed as funds disbursed from loans and aid are embezzled or handed out to inferior contractors who have won their bids through corrupt means (kickbacks, bribery, nepotism, etc.). Furthermore, investment in physical capital and human capital is reduced as resources are diverted from their most beneficial use.

Poverty and inequality

Corruption is generally not the weapon of the weak. In Nigeria, an (in)famous bribery case, involving the international oil company Shell, deprived Nigerian people of over $1.1 billion as the money went to corrupt officials instead of to the national budget Meanwhile, according to the World Bank (2019), more than 50% of the population of the oil-rich country live in extreme poverty. This example shows that as political and economic systems are enlisted in the service of corrupt actors, wealth is redistributed to the least needy sources. Mechanisms such as political representation and economic efficiency are both compromised by self-dealing and secret exchanges. Under conditions of corruption, funding for education, health care, poverty relief, and elections and political parties' operating expenses can become a source of personal enrichment for party officials, bureaucrats and contractors. Social programs and the redistributive potential of political systems suffer accordingly. A key result of all the instances named above is a state of unequal opportunity in which advantages arise only for those within a corrupt network.

Personal loss, intimidation and inconvenience

When people experience corruption, it is rarely a positive experience. A bribe must be paid to receive medical attention, obtain a building permit, pick up a package, or enjoy phone services. A judge rules against a party, not based on the facts of the case, but because the opponent paid a bribe, knows a power broker, or comes from the same racial or ethnic background. A person is beaten, detained or subject to a higher fine because he or she refuses to pay a bribe solicited by a police officer. Retirement funds are lost to fraudsters or tied up in a money-laundering scheme. While the victims of corruption suffer personal loss, intimidation and inconvenience, those who perpetrate corrupt acts and schemes tend to experience personal gain, a sense of superiority and greater convenience - pending enforcement of the law, that is.

Public and private sector dysfunctionality

The cumulative effect of individual corrupt acts is dysfunctionality. Whether offered by the public or private sectors, the quality of goods and services decrease, and the process of obtaining them becomes more expensive, time consuming and unfair. If bribes can successfully be offered to police, doctors, and civil servants, then those who are most successful at extracting these funds get ahead to the detriment of more honest colleagues and competitors who may perform better on merit. Moreover, corporations lose the incentive to offer better services and products if they can undermine competitors through obtaining political favors. State-owned enterprises and industries are structured to enrich government officials instead of pursuing innovation and efficiencies. This can lead to the loss of intrinsic motivation within organizations. Workers and managers are demoralized. People begin to doubt the value of hard work and innovation.

Failures in infrastructure

When a bridge collapsed in Genoa in August 2018, killing at least 39 people, there were many possible causes to consider Corruption was not the most obvious one, but subsequent investigations have found that a Mafia-controlled construction company appears to have used "weakened cement" in the building process. It is widely known that the construction industry is a valuable source of profits and a channel for money-laundering operations by the Mafia (additional information on organized crime can be found. Oversight and competition are both undermined in industries and firms plagued by organized corruption. Relatedly, a 2017 report by Mexicans against Corruption and Impunity blames corruption for the collapse of over 40 buildings during the September 2017 earthquake in Mexico City. Land-use and permit laws appear to have been bypassed, ostensibly through bribery, cronyism and influence trading, leading to the presence of fundamentally unsafe buildings around the capital.

Rigged economic and political systems

What is described as dysfunctional above is actually functional and profitable for corrupt actors. Whether falling under the label of political cronyism, crony capitalism, political party cartels, oligarchy, plutocracy and even, widespread patterns of private and public corruption construct social systems that are rigged in the private interest. Citizens with strong ethical principles (and citizens who lack significant funds, connections, favors to dispense, "hard power" over others such as guns or private enforcers) lose representation, influence and power.

Impunity and partial justice

When corruption pervades the justice system, people can no longer count on prosecutors and judges to do their jobs. The powerful may escape justice. And citizens, especially those with few resources or few powerful allies, may be unfairly accused of crimes, deprived of due process, and wrongly imprisoned. Resources on preventing corruption and strengthening integrity in the judiciary are available on the website of

Rising illiberal populism

and several scholarly publications make the point that increasing authoritarianism is partly fueled by corruption from 2017 by Faliscan as well as the resources referenced in In a nutshell, corruption increases inequality, decreases popular accountability and political responsiveness, and thus produces rising frustration and hardship among citizens, who are then more likely to accept (or even demand) hard-handed and illiberal tactics. Those tactics shift the blame for economic insecurity and political decline onto immigrants or other minority groups, and onto economic and political elites, who must, the theory goes, be dealt with swiftly and decisively. The rule of law and liberal values of tolerance and human dignity then become obstacles to needed change. For a more general discussion of values.

Organized crime and terrorism

Nefarious elements in society thrive as proceeds can be laundered, funding disguised, and judicial officials and politicians corrupted through bribes (including gifts, favors and other benefits). Levels of violence, illegal drugs, prostitution, sexual slavery, kidnapping and intimidation rise accordingly. The causal arrow goes in both directions. Not only does organized crime cause corruption, but opportunities for corruption left open by a weak, negligent or incapable State can also lead to organized crime. For a further discussion about the corruption-organized.

Diminished state capacity

Even if citizens were to adamantly demand that the problems listed above be addressed, corruption undermines the power of politics. For example, to the extent that bribery, trading in influence and state capture are widespread, political systems become incapable of addressing social problems whose resolution would threaten vested interests. Naturally, this is never acknowledged as such from within - state incapacity may manifest in a great many distracting and misleading ways, such as wedge issues, political party restructuring, the emergence of scandals and overwhelming outside issues that detract from structural problems, and so on. Under conditions of state capture, political arbitrage can be expected to occur in a highly strategic fashion. Issues will be played off against each other in order to frustrate systemic reforms. Moreover, as, corruption compromises the ethos of public service and changes political culture so as to render meaningful, public-spirited reforms virtually unthinkable.

Increasing polarization and unrest

When corruption, in particular state capture, becomes the norm, this can lead to polarization among citizens: those in support of corrupt regimes (because of kickbacks and handouts) versus those opposed to them. In the presence of diametrically opposed groups in society, compromise and reasoned discussion diminish. Policy is judged not on the basis of ideology or a project's inherent merits, but on who the policy proponents are and what benefits competing networks can reap.

Climate change and damage to biodiversity

Corruption derails anti-climate change funding and initiatives, defeats forest conservation and sustainable forest management programs, and fuels wildlife and fishery crimes These and other adverse effects of corruption on climate change and the environment are underscored in a TI report from 2011 and additional TI publications. On a broader level, the book *This Changes Everything* by Naomi Klein (2014) details how state capture by monies interests has derailed legislative efforts to address climate change in the United States. Her analysis applies to many countries around the world, given the power of the fossil fuels and automotive industries over governments - elected and unelected - across the globe. The perilous impact of corruption on the fisheries sector is discussed in detail in the publication while the report reveals how corruption enables criminal networks to illegally harvest timber in Peru.

Human rights violations

The observation that corrupt rulers tend to view civil liberties as obstacles to the consolidation of power can be traced back to many historical sources, including the collection of eighteenth century essays on corruption and tyranny known as *Cato's Letters*. Most recently of all, perhaps, the United Nations Office of the High Commission for Human Rights (OHCHR) has noted significant connections between corruption and human rights violations. Not only do those who report and oppose corruption end up on the receiving end of assassinations and human rights violations of many kinds, but also corruption itself decreases State capacity to address violations of civil and political rights and to make the necessary provisions to guarantee such rights, including socioeconomic rights, which often require complex initiatives on the part of governments. Corruption "a structural obstacle to the enjoyment of human rights" and has detailed many intersections between these two areas. For a further discussion and academic references.

Armed conflict and atrocity crimes

The diminished State capacity and development, brought about by corruption, can lead to insecurity and even armed conflict indeed, corruption has been recognized as a destabilizing factor and ultimately a "driver of conflict. Although the causal link between corruption and atrocity crimes (including genocide, war crimes and crimes against humanity) may be hard to prove, transitional justice mechanisms have identified corruption as a root cause of conflict and atrocity. See, for example the Sierra Leone Truth and Reconciliation Commission Report and the Liberian Truth and Reconciliation Commission Consolidated Final Report . In post-Arab Spring Tunisia, corruption was recognized as a root cause of the conflict even before the transitional justice mechanism operated. Thus, Tunisia's Law on Transitional Justice from 2013 (see English translation here) and the Truth and Dignity Commission that was created by the law were intended to establish accountability for the country's legacy of rampant corruption and human rights violations and to help reform the institutions that engaged in such crimes. Another relevant example is a 2018 report from the Open Society Justice Initiative, which offers evidence linking corruption to crimes against humanity in Mexico. For a further discussion and academic references about the corruption-conflict Anti-Corruption.

Public frustration and cynicism

People lose trust in leaders, in social systems (public institutions) and sometimes even in society and ethics itself when they sense that corruption is widespread and corrupt actors are not being held accountable. When political non-accountability increases, such perceptions persist for protracted periods and political participation diminishes. Moreover, public frustration and the sense that corruption is widespread can in turn pave the way for citizens themselves to take part in corrupt transactions, as discussed in a blog post on the Taxi Driver Paradox. In other words, social norms could encourage corrupt behavior as people tend to think that "if everybody is doing it, I might as well do it too." Failure to meet public expectations for zero-tolerance of corruption may have deleterious consequences for the legitimacy of State institutions and the very utility of formal norms that citizens and firms are expected to follow, possibly resulting in higher public tolerance of un-civic and free-riding behavior.

The effects of corruption mentioned above can be categorized along the following lines: economic, political, moral or psychological, humanitarian, ecological, security-related, and so on. To help us gain a better understanding of corruption, the following section discusses some of the deeper meanings of corruption.

Codes of conduct

Corruption prevention mechanisms often start with rules that prohibit certain types of conduct. Rules include legal prohibitions against corruption, and criminal and civil penalties directed at both the public and private sectors (Williams-Ellerbe, 2012), but also include codes of conduct and ethics for public officials. According to article 8 of UNCAC, such codes are to be used for promotion of personal standards (integrity, honesty and responsibility) and professional responsibilities for correct, impartial, honorable and proper performance of public functions. Codes provide guidance on how public officials should conduct themselves in relation to these standards and how they may be held accountable for their actions and decisions. In addition to UNCAC, other initiatives of regional and international organizations also recognize and promote the implementation of codes of conduct. An example of this is the International Code of Conduct for Public Officials, adopted by the UN General Assembly in 1996.

Systems of rewards and incentives

At a basic level, all countries should establish a system that rewards appropriate behavior and penalizes corrupt behavior in the public sector. The system should include extrinsic motivations such as a decent wage and merit-based appointments and promotions. Research compiled by the United States Agency for International Development (USAID, 2017) suggests that an invariable link between lower wages for public officials and corruption does not exist in all countries, but that, in some cases, higher wages and merit-based promotions are associated with a lower probability of the acceptance of illegal payments. In terms of intrinsic motivations, a high staff morale is crucial for anti-corruption efforts to succeed, and there is a lower tolerance for corruption among persons who find their jobs satisfying (Kwon 2014). Penalties for corrupt behavior are included in the anti-corruption laws of many countries, and research has shown that, in some cases, higher or harsher penalties for corrupt behaviors can lead to a decrease in public sector corruption (Foilsman and Miguel, 2007; Hasty, 2005).

Accessibility

This refers to the ability of all firms to access government contract opportunities (OECD, 2016). Full accessibility is required to increase competition in public procurement and foster the participation of small and medium-sized enterprises (SMEs) in public procurement. Access is fostered by reducing the bureaucracy inherent in the tender process, cutting the cost of participation in public procurement and streamlining the tender process. Limiting bureaucracy is particularly important in public procurement. Access to public contracts by SMEs and other target companies can be facilitated by rules requiring a portion of government contracts to be awarded to SMEs, women, minorities and other target groups.

Human resources management

The rules and procedures for hiring, rotation, promotion, professionalization, and training of civil servants also play a role in the combating of corruption in the public sector. For example, staff rotation in jobs that are vulnerable to corruption is expected to assist in preventing corrupt relationships from forming and in disrupting established corrupt relationships. Rotation may also lead to reduced incentives to engage in corruption for private sector actors, as there might not be the future guarantee of the corrupt partner's continuation in a particular position. Merit-based recruiting is another example of a human resources management system designed to disrupt corruption. Article 7 of UNCAC stipulates that the human resources management system of the civil service must be based on the underlying principles of transparency, integrity and efficiency. This includes ensuring the prevalence of objective criteria for the recruitment, retention, promotion and retirement of public officials, as well as continuous learning opportunities and adequate and equitable remuneration and conditions of employment for staff in the civil service. As with all anti-corruption measures, rotation must be balanced against other concerns, such as building competency and commitment to public service.

Citizen and stakeholder participation

Public sector accountability requires that a wide range of stakeholders - such as anti-corruption offices, private sector organizations, end-users, civil society, academia, the media and the general public - participates in public sector processes and in the procurement process in particular (OECD, 2016). Participation of citizens is especially important in this regard, including in the procurement context (Heroes, 2012; Lindell-Mills, 2013). In some countries, recognition of the importance of citizen participation in public procurement processes is reflected in the law. For example, laws in Mongolia and Mexico call for citizen participation in public procurement processes (Paraffin, 2015). This has shown to be effective in Mexico in terms of reducing the cost of public contracts (De Simone and Shah, 2012). Citizen participation in anti-corruption efforts is discussed in detail in Module 10 of the E4J University Module Series on Anti-Corruption.

Open government and e-government

Requires States to adopt procedures for public reporting and access to public sector information. In this regard, many countries have established e-government services that allow the use of information and communication technologies in connection with government functions and procedures, with the purpose of increasing efficiency, transparency and citizen participation can improve the delivery of public services, build trust between citizens and government, and contribute to public sector reform initiatives. Is actively used to promote integrity particularly in public procurement and management of public finances as it can strengthen transparency, facilitate access to public tenders and simplify administrative procedures Moreover, Reduce direct interaction between procurement officials and companies ... and allow for easier detection of irregularities and corruption, such as bid rigging schemes. The digitalization of procurement processes strengthens internal anti-corruption controls and detection of integrity breaches, and it provides audit services trails that may facilitate investigation activities.

A good example of promoting access to information is the Open Data Charter, which as of September 2019 has been adopted by 71 national and local governments across the world, although there are disproportionately few signatories from non-Western countries (see current list of nations), and endorsed by 49 organizations from civil society and private sectors. Government information shared as part of the Open Data Charter should comply with six principles: the data should be

- open by default
- timely
- comprehensible
- accessible and useable
- comparable; and
- Interoperable (following international data standards).

- The data should be designed to foster improved governance and citizen engagement, and it should promote inclusive development and innovation the Another example of a country that has adopted the Open Data Charter is Ukraine where an online and open data system was launched in 2015 to ensure that documents and information related to public procurement would be easily accessible to civil society. has had a measurable impact on saving the government millions of euros and increasing bidding on contracts by 50 per cent In terms of public procurement, the European Union has adopted which requires publishing all public tenders above a certain contract value in the *Supplement to the Official Journal of such* legal requirements and efforts to provide open information platforms are critical to preventing opportunities for corruption.

To assist in providing governments with support and technical knowledge on how to implement open data initiatives, offers numerous resources and training programs. For example, showcases the use of open data to promote and enforce anti-corruption efforts. An example of how used by individual countries is the public information database. The website provides a vast range of information from all public institutions in Georgia, including planned expenditures, bonuses and salaries of civil servants, increasing transparency in public activities and allowing citizens and non-governmental institutions (NGOs) to better understand and study the public spending by the Georgian authorities.

Managing conflicts of interest

Conflicts of interest could lead to corruption, therefore such conflicts need to be disclosed and addressed in a manner that will prevent a descent into corruption. In general, conflicts of interest are addressed through financial and asset disclosure requirements, codes of conduct and other regulations, such as prohibiting public officials to work in the private sector for a certain period of time after they leave the public service. The purpose of these measures is to require public officials to recuse themselves from decisions where an actual or potential conflict may arise

Most of the modern asset and interest disclosure systems were developed following the adoption in response to the requirements of article 8 of the Convention to avoid potential conflicts of interest in the future, facilitate the management of such conflicts and ensure that corrupt public officials will not be able to conceal the proceeds of any illegal activity The open data measures, which were discussed in the section above, can also be used to facilitate the proceeding of asset declarations for public officials. Additionally, making information easily available on topics such as asset declarations and the tender process in public procurement encourages journalists and researchers to scrutinize data and sectors of society that are often vulnerable to corruption. For more information on how asset declarations can be

Compliance-friendly environment

In relation to ensuring compliance with anti-corruption rules and norms in the public sector, nudges and training programs are common ways of creating an environment for compliance.), who defined it as:

Any aspect of the choice architecture that alters people's behavior in a predictable way without forbidding any options or significantly changing their economic incentives. To count as a mere nudge, the intervention must be easy to implement and cost effective. Nudges are not mandates. Putting fruit at eye level counts as a nudge. Banning junk food does not.

Nudge theory presumes that, when faced with a choice, people are more likely to go for a default option, and so presenting simple alternatives at the moment of decision-making can alter behavior without heavy-handed enforcement.

In the corruption context, the concept of ambient accountability takes nudge theory a little further and uses "physical space and the built environment to empower people, help them understand/assert their rights and stop corruption right where it matters - ideas, inspiration, evidence from stickers, murals and billboards, to feedback interfaces, urban screens and architectural interventions" Anti-corruption and ethics training are common in the public sector and in specialized areas like public procurement - the idea being to sensitize officials to the rules, to areas of risk and to measures to take when faced with ethical dilemmas Integrity and ethics management is further discussed.

Monitoring and oversight

Monitoring can take the form of audits, transparency measures that provide information needed to hold the public sector to account and civil society monitoring. Research by Di Tell and demonstrates that audits on public hospitals in Argentina reduced the cost of medical supplies by 15 per cent, Fuertes and show that audits reduced municipal corruption by The kind and nature of oversight over, for instance, the procurement process depends on a risk assessment of the procurement environment. Control measures can thus serve as risk management tools as long as they are "coherent and include effective and clear procedures for responding to credible suspicions of violations of laws and regulations, and facilitate reporting to the competent authorities without fear of reprisals

Accountability and scrutiny (the four-eye principle)

The four-eye principle refers to a requirement that some public sector activities or decisions must be approved by at least two people. The four-eye principle is a tool for monitoring and increased accountability and operates on the basis that it is harder to corrupt two people than one person although this might not be the case in systemically corrupt societies.

In the 1990s corruption was increasingly perceived to have a negative impact on economy, democracy, and the rule of law, as was pointed out by Kofi Annan. Those effects claimed by Annan could be proven by a variety of empirical studies, as reported by Juli Bacio Terrac. The increased awareness of corruption was widespread and shared across professional, political, and geographical borders. While an international effort against corruption seemed to be unrealistic during the Cold War, a new discussion on the global impact of corruption became possible, leading to an official condemnation of corruption by governments, companies, and various other stakeholders. The 1990s additionally saw an increase in press freedom, the activism of civil societies, and global communication through an improved communication infrastructure, which paved the way to a more thorough understanding of the global prevalence and negative impact of corruption. In consequence to those developments, international non-governmental organizations (e.g. Transparency International) and inter-governmental organizations and initiatives (e.g. the OECD Working group on bribery) were founded to overcome corruption.

Since the 2000s, the discourse became broader in scope. It became more common to refer to corruption as a violation of human rights, which was also discussed by the responsible international bodies. Besides attempting to find a fitting description for corruption, the integration of corruption into a human rights-framework was also motivated by underlining the importance of corruption and educating people on its costs

International law

Approaching the fight against corruption in an international setting is often seen as preferential over addressing it exclusively in the context of the nation state. The reasons for such preference are multidimensional, ranging from the necessary international cooperation for tracing international corruption scandals, to the binding nature of international treaties, and the loss in relative competitiveness by outlawing an activity that remains legal in other countries.

In national and in international legislation, there are laws interpreted as directed against corruption. The laws can stem from resolutions of international organizations, which are implemented by the national governments, who are ratifying those resolutions or be directly issued by the respective national legislative.

Laws against corruption are motivated by similar reasons that are generally motivating the existence of criminal law, as those laws are thought to, on the one hand, bring justice by holding individuals accountable for their wrongdoing, justice can be achieved by sanctioning those corrupted individuals, and potential criminals are deterred by having the consequences of their potential actions demonstrated to them

While bribing domestic officials was criminalized in most countries even before the ratification of international conventions and treaties, many national law systems did not recognize bribing foreign officials, or more sophisticated methods of corruption, as illegal. Only after ratifying and implementing above mentioned conventions the illegal character of those offenses was fully recognized. Where legislation existed prior to the ratification of the OECD convention, the implementation resulted in an increased compliance with the legal framework.

Corruption is often addressed by specialized investigative or prosecution authorities, often labelled as anti-corruption agencies (ACA), that are tasked with varying duties and subject to varying degrees of independence .